ENDOCRINE SYSTEM

LORRIE KLOSTERMAN

mc Marshall Cavendish
Benchmark
New York

Marshall Cavendish Benchmark
99 White Plains Road
Tarrytown, New York 10591
www.marshallcavendish.us

All Web sites were available and accurate when this book was sent to press.

Editor: Karen Ang
Publisher: Michelle Bisson
Art Director: Anahid Hamparian
Series Designer: Kay Petronio

Library of Congress Cataloging-in-Publication Data
Klosterman, Lorrie.
Endocrine system / by Lorrie Klosterman.
p. cm. -- (The amazing human body)
Includes bibliographical references and index.
Summary: "Discusses the parts that make up the human endocrine system, what can go wrong, how to treat those illnesses
and diseases, and how to stay healthy"--Provided by publisher.
ISBN 978-0-7614-3055-1
1. Endocrine glands--Juvenile literature. I. Title.
QP187.K66 2009
612.4--dc22
2007050444

This book is not intended for use as a substitute for advice, consultation, or treatment by a licensed medical practitioner. The reader is advised that no action of a medical nature should be taken without consultation with a licensed medical practitioner, including action that may seem to be indicated by the contents of this work, since individual circumstances vary and medical standards, knowledge, and practices change with time. The publisher, author, and medical consultants disclaim all liability and cannot be held responsible for any problems that may arise from use of this book.

 = cells from the thyroid, an organ that is part of the endocrine system

Front cover: The organs of the endocrine system
Title page: A cell from the pituitary, an endocrine organ
Back cover: Melatonin, a hormone
Front cover photo: © MedicalRF.com/Alamy
Photo research by Tracey Engel

The photographs in this book are used by permission and through the courtesy of:
Credits: Alamy: PHOTOTAKE Inc., 2, 9, 10, 11, 19, 21, 22, 32, 33, 38, 40, 60, 63, back cover; Bryan & Cherry Alexander Photography, 23; Nucleus Medical Art, Inc., 24, 34; MedicalRF.com, 26, 28; David J. Green, 31; Angela Hampton Picture Library, 35, Mark Downey, 41; Chris Pancewicz, 42; Martin Shields, 48; Medical-on-Line, 53, 57; David White, 58; Arco Images, 62; JUPITERIMAGES/Brand X, 70; Photo Researchers, Inc.: Michael Ross, 6; Alfred Pasieka, 14; James Cavallini, 16; Quest, 17; Anatomical Travelogue, 25; Prof. K. Seddon & Dr. T. Evans, QUB, 29; John Bavosi, 50; Mehau Kulyk, 52; Miriam Maslo, 54; Russ Curtis, 55; Ton Kinsbergen, 68; Superstock: Image Source Black, 7, 12; Shutterstock: Sebastian Kaulitzki, 13; Eugene Bochkarev, 47; Karin Lau, 49; Tischenko Irina, 65; Denis Pepin, 66; Mandy Godbehear, 67; Alistair Scott, 69; Phototake: Nucleus Medical Art, Inc., 44; Getty Images: Tim Boyle, 45.

Printed in China
23456

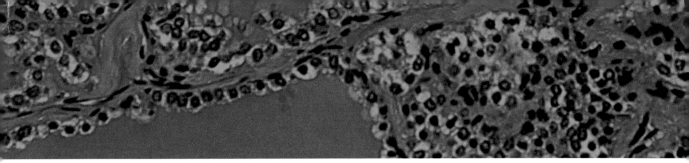

CONTENTS

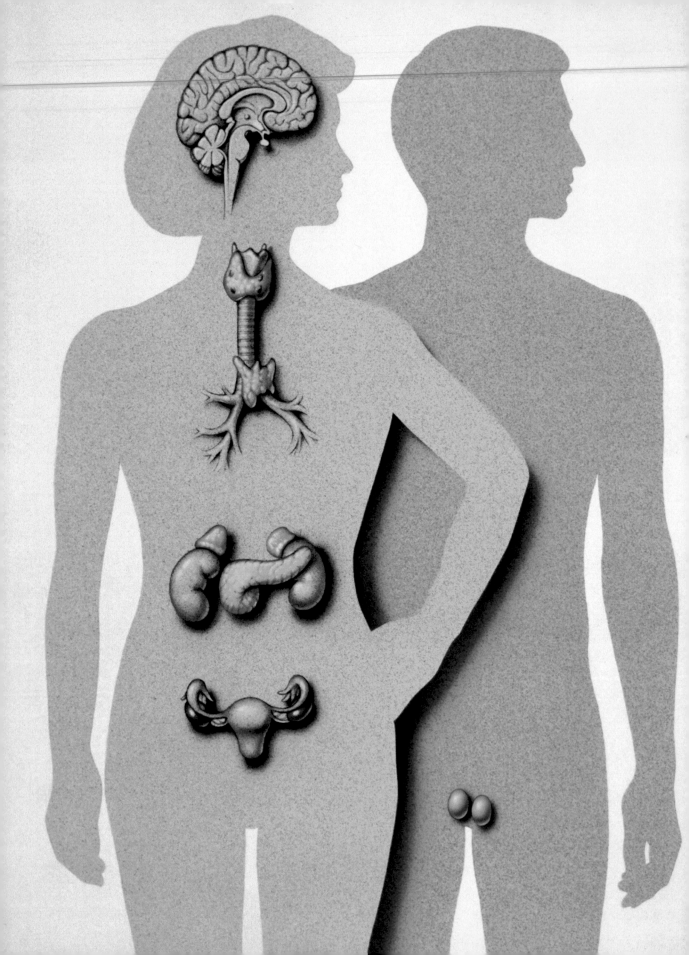

1

What Is the Endocrine System?

Have you ever wondered why a young person's body changes so much during the teenage years? Or why a grown man looks so much different from a woman? Or perhaps you know someone who must have a shot of a certain medication each day for a medical condition called diabetes. Maybe you have heard of a famous athlete who was kicked off a sports team for taking steroids to boost athletic ability.

In each of these examples, the endocrine system plays a role. The endocrine system is a collection of cells that controls much of what the human body does. It helps a person grow properly from a tiny baby into an adult. It helps people turn the foods we eat into energy so we can move, play, think, and much more. The endocrine system makes sure

Men and women have most of the same endocrine organs. The only ones that are different are their reproductive organs.

important substances in the bloodstream are present in the right amounts to maintain good health. Even the creation of new life—a baby—would not be possible without the endocrine system.

CELLS AND ORGANS

The activities of the endocrine system rely on a wide variety of cells. Cells are the tiniest living things and can only be seen with the aid of a microscope. The human body is made of trillions of cells. There are hundreds of different kinds. Cells of the same kind group together into structures that we can see with the naked eye. For instance, certain types of cells form layers that cover our bodies in skin. And a different type

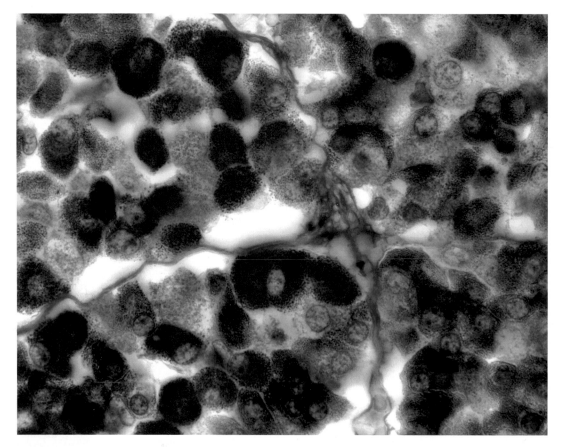

Many tiny cells form the pituitary gland—a very important endocrine organ located in the brain.

of cell groups together into muscles, just beneath the skin. Some groups of cells belong to the endocrine system.

Many parts of the body are called organs. An organ is a collection of cells of many different kinds, which all work together to carry out some task. The eyes are organs that allow us to see. The stomach is an organ that digests food. The heart is an organ that pumps blood through blood vessels. Some organs are part of the endocrine system.

ENDOCRINE CELLS EVERYWHERE

Cells of the endocrine system are found in many places of the body. Some are scattered in small clusters among other types of cells. For instance, endocrine cells are present along the digestive tract—the

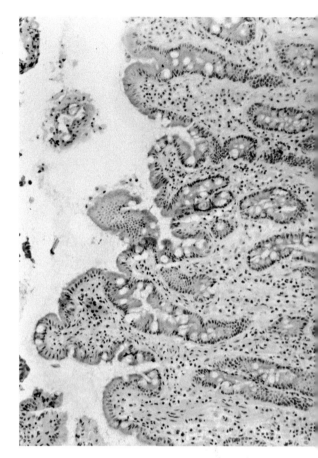

A person's digestive system could not function properly without endocrine cells and organs. This image has been magnified thousands of times to show some of the cells in the digestive tract.

path along which food travels, including the mouth, throat, esophagus, stomach, and intestine. Most cells along the digestive tract break up food into tiny particles that get into the bloodstream. The endocrine cells in the digestive tract help to control the activities of the food-digesting cells.

Other endocrine cells are in special endocrine organs that mostly help control the body's activities. Examples of endocrine organs are the thyroid (in the neck), the pancreas (in the abdomen near the stomach), the pair of adrenal glands (one on top of each kidney), and the pituitary gland (within the brain).

Some people like to refer to an endocrine organ as a gland—the thyroid gland, pituitary gland, adrenal glands, and so on. A gland is any structure of the body that produces a substance, usually as a liquid. The liquids made by endocrine glands, or organs, are released inside the body in tiny amounts. They are called hormones.

HORMONES

There are thousands of important chemicals in the body, but only some have earned the name "hormone." To be a hormone, a chemical must be made in one part of the body, and then travel to another part of the body through the bloodstream to cause cells in that second area to change somehow. A hormone made by the pituitary gland, for instance, changes what cells in the liver are doing. (The liver is an organ in the abdomen, on the right side, partly protected by ribs.) Another hormone, made by the tiny parathyroid glands in the neck region, changes how much calcium is stored away by cells in the bones. Yet another hormone made by the pancreas influences what becomes of sugars that we eat.

Target Cells

Certain cells will react to a hormone, but other cells will not. The cells that do are target cells of that hormone. The name "target cells" makes it sound as though a hormone is aiming for them, as if the hormone knows just where to go. This is not the case. Hormones are carried from an endocrine cell to all cells by the bloodstream. Wherever blood goes, hormones go. Hormones are able to slip out of tiny blood vessels and drift around in the moist areas between cells. Some hormones—the ones called steroids, which are made of lipids, or fats—are even able to go inside cells.

While drifting around or inside cells, a hormone may suddenly stop for a moment. It has stuck to a cell by some attractive force. This is because it has bumped into a receptor.

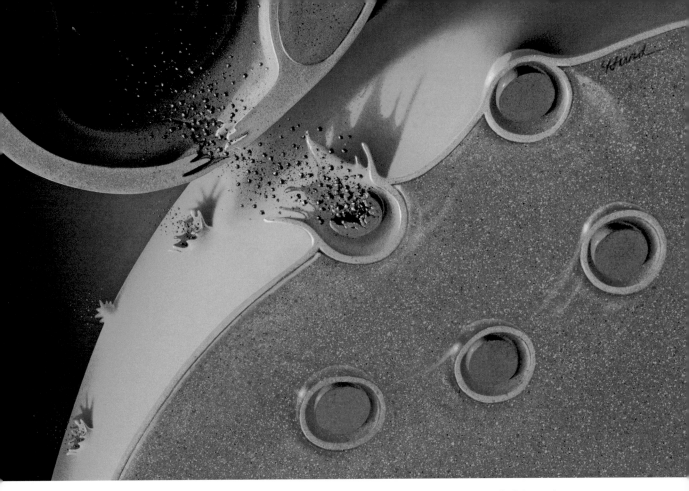

Endocrine hormones (purple) are released into the bloodstream where they are carried throughout the body.

Receptors for Hormones

A receptor is a physical structure—a very tiny one—on the surface or interior of a cell. For a fraction of a second, the hormone comes into contact with the receptor. In that moment, the hormone is attached, or bound, to the cell.

Receptors are made of protein and are built by the target cells. Only a cell that makes and has receptors for hormones will be a target, because only those cells will be able to hold hormones. Every target cell has dozens or hundreds of copies of the same kind of receptor. That way the hormone can bind to the cell in many places. This strengthens the message from the hormone to the target cell. In addition, cells have many kinds of receptors, so they can respond to different kinds of hormones.

Estrogen is a hormone made by the ovaries, which are part of a woman's reproductive system.

PICKY RECEPTORS

If you have ever been in the school's band room, or known someone who plays a musical instrument, you know that each type of instrument has its own type of carrying case. A trumpet fits into a trumpet case. A trombone fits well into a trombone case.

The same can be said for a hormone and a receptor. Just like a trombone needs a case that accommodates its size and shape, a hormone needs a specific receptor that it can match up to. Each type of hormone will only bind to the receptor it matches.

Cell Response

How does a hormone "tell" a target cell what to do? The answer to this question is very complex, but the simple answer is in these three steps:

- A hormone attaches to its receptor.
- The receptor changes its shape slightly to hold the hormone.
- That change in shape causes a chain reaction of activity inside the cell.

A chain reaction occurs when one event or action leads to another and then another and so on. Maybe you have enjoyed setting dominoes or cards on their ends in a long row, so that if you tap one, it falls, knocking over all the others in sequence. This is something like what goes on inside a cell after a hormone binds to a receptor.

But what does a cell *do* for its activity? That depends on what type of cell it is, and what hormone is attached. Often, a hormone will make a cell produce more of a substance, or less of a substance. For instance, when a growth hormone binds to it, a muscle cell might make more of the

This illustration shows the basic structure of a molecule of melatonin, a hormone that controls sleep cycles. The structure and shape of the hormone molecules fit exactly into their specific cell receptors—like a lock and key.

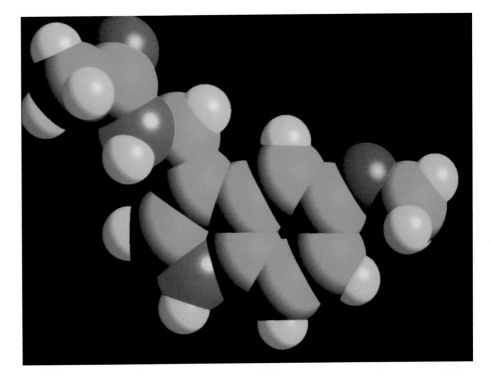

proteins it uses to change shape. Or the muscle cell will take in more sugar from the bloodstream when the hormone insulin binds to it. A fat cell will carry out chemical reactions to store away sugars as fat when the insulin binds to it.

The End of a Hormone

After a hormone sticks to a receptor and causes the reaction, the hormone comes off, and is soon destroyed—perhaps within seconds! Enzymes in cells or in the bloodstream quickly break down each hormone molecule into an inactive form. This is called hormone metabolism. Liver cells are especially good at hormone metabolism, breaking down those that arrive in the bloodstream. Ending a hormone molecule's activity rapidly allows for minute-to-minute control of a cell's activities. If more activity is needed, more hormone is quickly released.

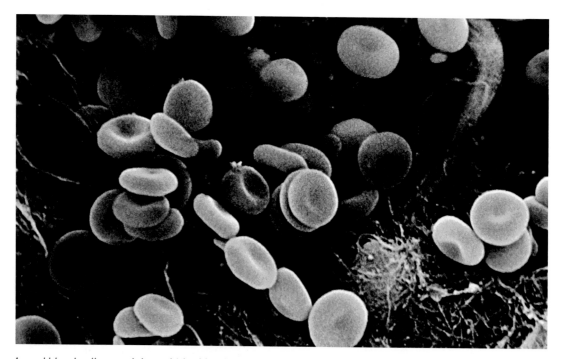

As red blood cells travel through the blood vessels around the body, they carry oxygen to all cells. The bloodstream is also a pathway for hormones and other important body chemicals.

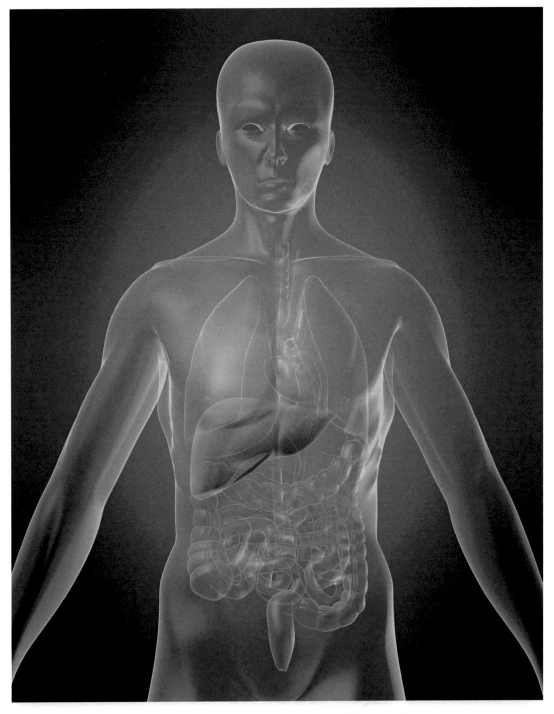

The liver, which is located just below the lungs and above most of the digestive organs, has many body functions. One of its most important activities is breaking down materials in the body, such as hormones and other body chemicals.

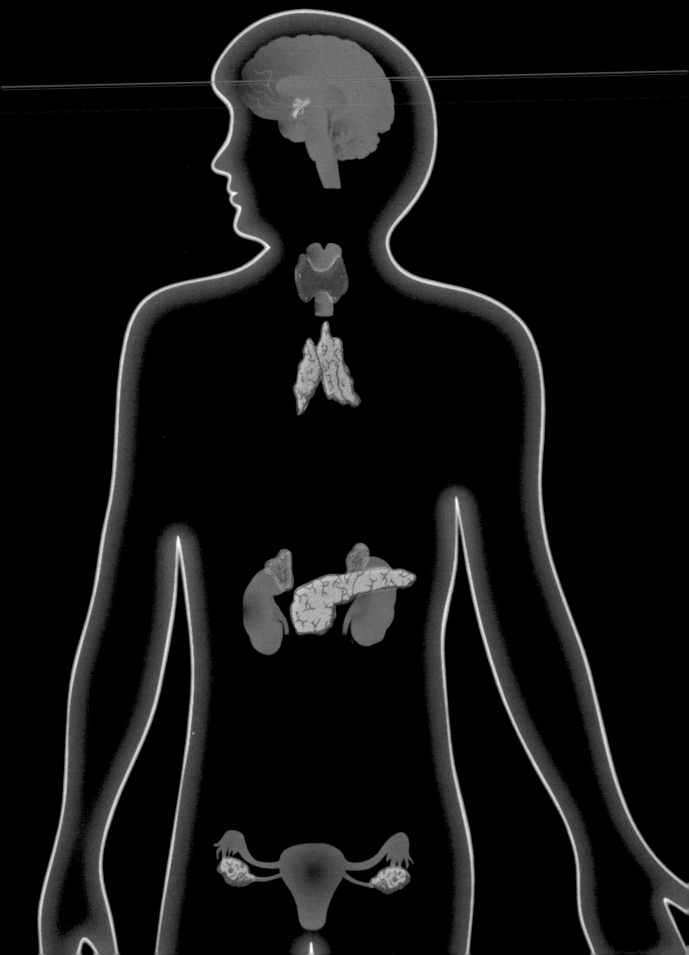

2

The Major Endocrine Organs

Every doctor and nurse, and every student who has studied the details of the human body, knows about the major endocrine organs. Most were discovered centuries ago, though their purposes were not always clear for many years. Now their main functions are known, but new discoveries about them are happening all the time.

THE POWERFUL PITUITARY

The pituitary—also known as the pituitary gland—is a powerful little organ. In adults, it is about the size of a small olive. The pituitary is

◄ *Endocrine organs, shown here in red, yellow, and orange, can be found in different parts of the body—from inside the brain to a person's reproductive organs.*

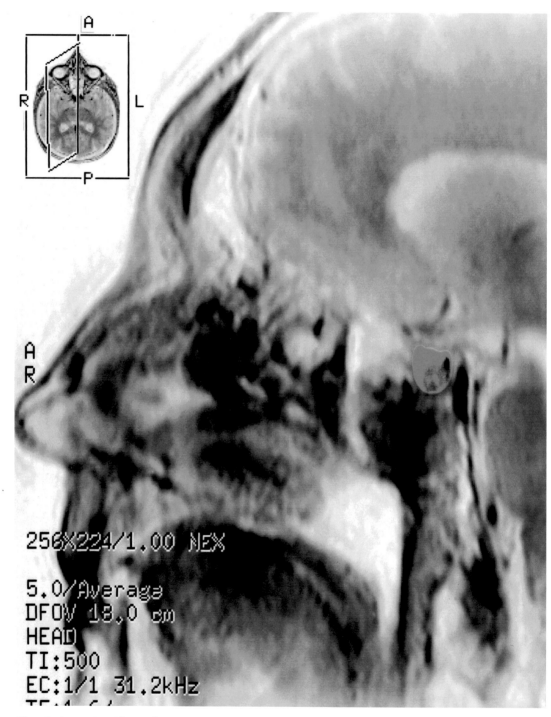

256X224/1.00 NEX

5.0/Average
DFOV 18.0 cm
HEAD
TI:500
EC:1/1 31.2kHz

The pituitary gland (green) is located deep inside the brain. It is small compared to other endocrine organs, but it controls many body functions.

nestled deep within the skull, against the underside of the brain. It makes many different hormones and controls many things, including growth, minerals, reproduction, energy usage by cells, and more.

Experts often talk about two parts of the pituitary, the anterior (front), and posterior (back). (There is also a middle portion of the pituitary, though the purpose of its hormones in people is not well understood.) Cells in the anterior part of the pituitary look similar to many other endocrine cells, but the posterior part contains only long, armlike extensions of nerve cells clustered in a nearby brain area. These "arms" release hormones made by the nerve cells.

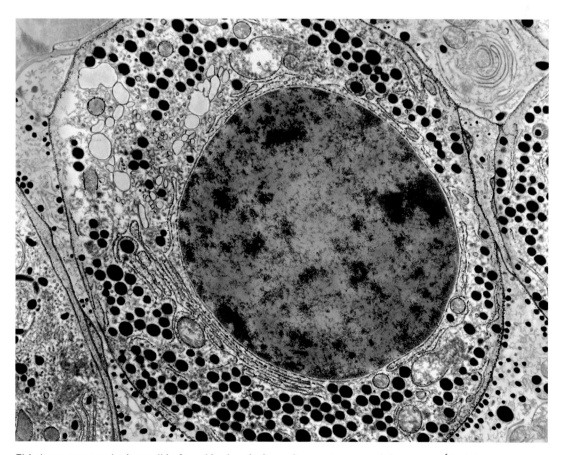

This hormone-producing cell is found in the pituitary. It secretes growth hormones (dark brown granules) that aid in body growth and development.

A good example of how important a hormone from this small gland can be is growth hormone (GH). The amount of GH made by the pituitary can determine if a person will be three feet tall or seven feet tall! (Although height also depends on nutrition, the height of parents, and other factors.) GH stimulates growth during childhood years in several ways. One way is getting cells that live within bones to make more bone material. Researchers have discovered that GH works on bone cells, but also causes the liver to make another hormone needed by growing bones. That hormone is IGF (insulinlike growth factor), which is made by several other kinds of cells in response to GH, too. GH is also necessary for a healthy body throughout life. It aids many kinds of cells in using nutrients they get from the bloodstream.

Another pituitary hormone, ADH (antidiuretic hormone), does something very different. It helps kidney cells to save water when a person is dehydrated, or low on internal fluids. Thanks to ADH, kidney cells are able to reclaim some water that would have been lost in urine.

The pituitary gets involved in reproduction, too, with the hormones prolactin and oxytocin. In a woman, prolactin is more plentiful than usual when she is pregnant, and for many months after her baby is born. Prolactin helps her breasts make milk. Oxytocin helps the breast move milk out while a baby is nursing. These two hormones also assist in other reproductive tasks throughout a woman's life, such as making ova, or eggs. In men, prolactin helps make healthy sperm.

Several pituitary hormones stimulate, or boost, other endocrine cells elsewhere in the body. The endocrine cells of the thyroid respond to TSH (thyroid stimulating hormone). The endocrine cells in gonads (ovaries in women, testes in men) respond to FSH (follicle-stimulating hormone) and LH (luteinizing hormone). Some of the endocrine cells in the adrenals respond to ACTH (adrenocorticotropic hormone).

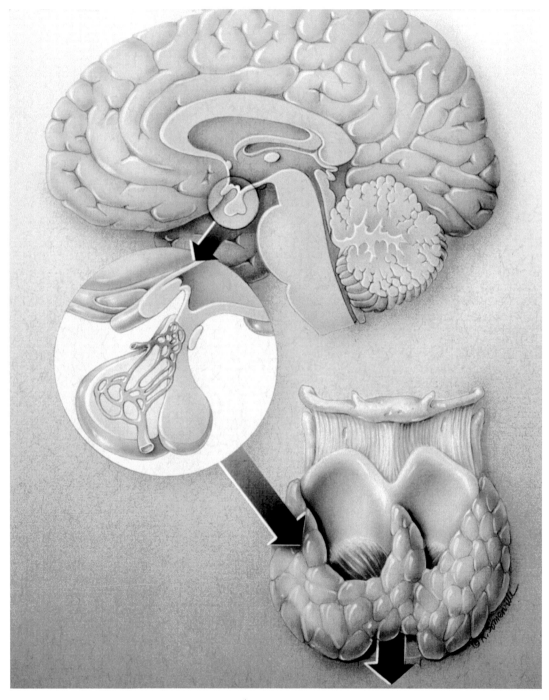

The pituitary gland also plays a part in controlling other endocrine organs. Some of the hormones secreted by the pituitary (top) direct certain thyroid functions (bottom).

FEEDBACK LOOPS

Have you ever been riding in a car and it was too cold? You turn on the heater, but soon it gets too hot, so you turn it down—until it gets too cold again, and you turn it up again. You are trying to get just the right temperature. In a similar way, endocrine organs "try" to make just the right amount of hormone for what the body needs at any moment. How do they "know" what amount of hormone is just right? They get feedback.

Feedback means knowing the results of an action. (The comments you get from a teacher on a homework assignment are a type of feedback.) Endocrine cells get feedback, too, in a process called a feedback loop. For example, aldosterone is made by the adrenals. Aldosterone causes kidney cells to save the important mineral sodium before it is lost in urine. But too much sodium is dangerous, so this is where feedback comes in. Adrenal cells can tell when the fluids around them have too much sodium. If that happens, they make less aldosterone. Less aldosterone means less sodium is saved by kidney cells. So, sodium in blood and tissues drops to a safer level.

Feedback loops can be much more complex than that example, such as among the hypothalamus, pituitary, and thyroid. Each one "keeps track" of how much hormone the others are making, and adjusts its own hormone output as needed.

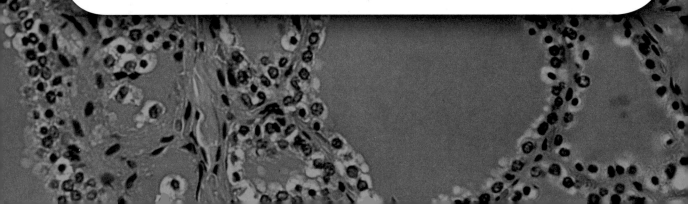

A HIGHER AUTHORITY:
THE HYPOTHALAMUS

For a long time the pituitary was called "the master gland" because some of its hormones control other endocrine cells. But it lost this title when researchers figured out that the pituitary is under the control of a nearby brain region called the hypothalamus. The hypothalamus produces many chemicals called releasing factors. Each releasing factor controls the release of a certain pituitary hormone.

The hypothalamus is in a great location to "know" how much of the pituitary hormones are needed to keep the body running smoothly. A lot of information from the surrounding brain comes to the hypothalamus. For instance, if it is cold and one's body temperature is falling, the hypothalamus receives this information from nearby brain cells, and it releases more of the factor that will stimulate the pituitary to release TSH. TSH stimulates the thyroid to release more thyroid hormones, and muscles respond to them by twitching, which causes shivering. That muscle action warms up the body.

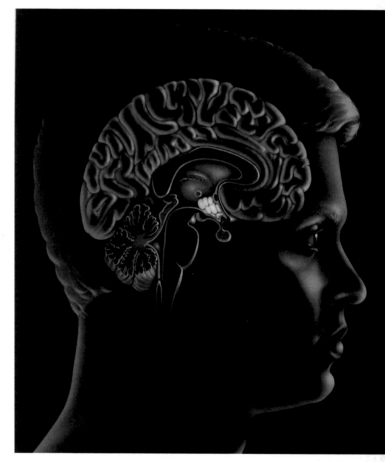

The hypothalamus is located near the center of the brain, and is involved with many body systems, including the endocrine system.

Scientists are still trying to figure out all the ways melatonin affects the body, but they do know that it can control sleep cycles and moods.

THE MYSTERIOUS PINEAL GLAND

Some endocrine organs are more mysterious than others, even today. The pineal is one. Researchers discovered many years ago that this gland, deep within the brain, makes the hormone melatonin. It is made mostly at night because light blocks its production. Melatonin is known to control reproduction in animals that have young only in spring and summer, when days are long and warm, and food plants are abundant. In these animals, melatonin prevents sperm and eggs from maturing during the dark winter months when food is scarce.

But what could melatonin do in people, who have babies all year round? Scientists are still working that out. It certainly seems important in making us sleepy at night. The hormone also appears to be a powerful antioxidant, or a type of substance that breaks apart harmful chemicals that build up in our bodies and damage our cells. Researchers are looking into whether melatonin might prevent cancer and slow aging.

LIGHTS, HORMONES, AND HAPPINESS

Do you ever feel especially tired, foggy, or unhappy during the fall or winter, for no clear reason? Many people feel that way. Some even become severely depressed. Since 1985, doctors have agreed there is a condition called seasonal affective disorder, or SAD. It is also called winter depression, winter blues, or the hibernation reaction. Melatonin, the pineal gland's hormone, may be to blame.

Melatonin is made during dim light and dark hours, and one of its effects is to make us sleepy and low on energy. That helps us get a good night's sleep. But in parts of the world where winter brings many more hours of darkness than daylight—as in the northeastern United States, Canada, and northern Europe—melatonin may get too abundant, causing daytime grogginess and fatigue. To make things worse, melatonin is made from serotonin, another brain chemical. That chemical is thought to help us feel happy. Serotonin's quantity gets lower at night, as some of it is made into melatonin. Together, the low serotonin and high melatonin create SAD symptoms.

SAD must be diagnosed by a medical professional. Certain medications that increase the amount of serotonin in the brain can help ease symptoms. Also, special lamps with bulbs that mimic the Sun's light help people with SAD get through the hormonal challenges of winter.

Some treatments for SAD include sitting in front of special lights that are supposed to help your body adjust its hormones.

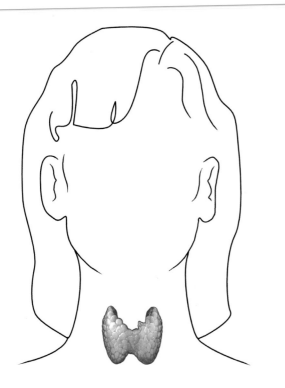
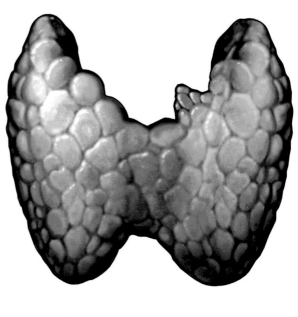

The thyroid is located at the base of the neck.

THYROID FOR ENERGY

Every waking moment, our cells are busily carrying out their tasks. Muscle cells are helping us move, lift things, run, and keep us upright in a chair. Immune cells are destroying germs. Stomach cells are making acid to digest food. Intestinal cells are shuttling the digested food molecules into the bloodstream. Cells are repairing themselves, and new cells are being formed to replace those that have died. Even while we sleep, many cells continue working. All this activity keeps us warm, too.

These cellular tasks would not go well without the thyroid's two hormones, T3 and T4. (The numerals 3 and 4 stand for the number of iodine atoms in each hormone.) The thyroid is located in the neck region and shaped somewhat like a bow tie. Its hormones are essential for a cell to properly use food particles for energy.

A very different hormone, calcitonin, comes from clusters of cells scattered throughout the thyroid. Calcitonin lowers the amount of calcium in the bloodstream and in the fluids around cells by getting bone cells to store away any excess as calcium phosphate, the hard material that makes bones strong. Calcium, in just the right amounts, is also essential for muscle contraction that allows us to move, and the heart to pump, and for nerves and the brain to work, and for many other tasks.

FOUR TINY PARATHYROIDS

Parathyroid means "next to the thyroid." The parathyroids are four pea-sized organs that hug the back surface of the thyroid. Their hormone, PTH (parathyroid hormone), keeps calcium from becoming too scarce.

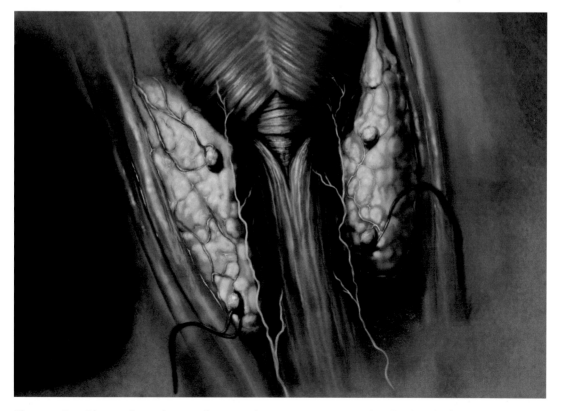

The parathyroids are shown here as four round structures connected to the thyroid tissue.

PTH gets cells of the intestine to absorb calcium from foods and beverages, and cells of the kidneys to absorb calcium from urine. PTH also triggers bone cells to take tiny amounts of calcium from calcium phosphate and put it into the bloodstream.

The two hormones, PTH and calcitonin, have opposite effects on calcium levels in the body. This is an excellent example of how the endocrine system keeps the amount of something—in this case calcium—just where a healthy body needs it to be.

THE PANCREAS AND FOOD PARTICLES

We all need food and beverages to keep our bodies going. Whatever we eat travels along the digestive tract and is broken down into microscopic

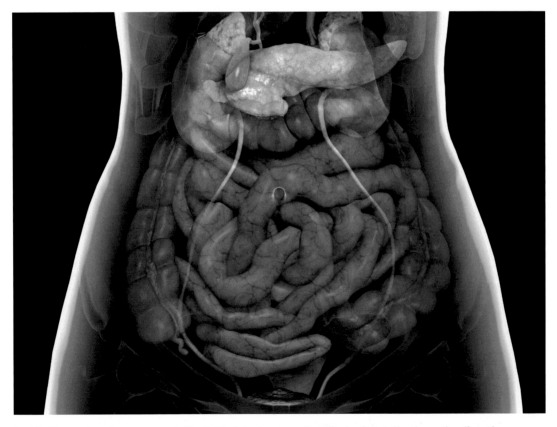

In this illustration, the pancreas is the light pink structure that sits horizontally above the digestive organs.

particles—sugars, amino acids (of which proteins are made), and lipids. Cells along the intestine move these particles into nearby blood vessels. The vessels then whisk the food particles away, taking them everywhere blood goes. In this way, all living cells get a supply of food they can use for energy.

But after a meal or sugary snack, there are more food particles in the bloodstream than the body needs at once. The extra food is stored by certain cells to be used later, between meals. Assisting in this process are two hormones of the pancreas—insulin and glucagon.

Insulin aids cells in taking food particles in to store them. The liver (a large organ in the abdomen), fat cells (scattered all over as "body fat"), and muscle cells are especially good at responding to insulin. They are like the cabinets in a kitchen where food is put away after grocery shopping.

Glucagon does the opposite of insulin. When the amount of food particles in the bloodstream is getting low, glucagon activates liver and fat cells to break down stored food particles and put them into the bloodstream, so all cells can use them. (Hormones from the adrenal glands do so, too.) The brain especially depends on glucagon for this, because brain cells cannot store food for themselves, yet they need energy all day long, and all night, too. Glucagon also helps someone who is exercising to continue fueling their muscles even if muscles' stored food is running low.

ADRENALS: A GLAND WITHIN A GLAND

The adrenals are a pair of organs inside the abdomen, one on the left and one on the right, cupping the top of each kidney. A central portion of each adrenal is called the medulla (like "middle"). Surrounding that is the larger cortex portion. Like the pituitary, the adrenal has typical hormone-secreting cells in the cortex, but neuronlike cells in the medulla.

You need to eat plenty of vitamins and minerals to stay healthy. One mineral that is very important is sodium. Sodium is quite abundant in our

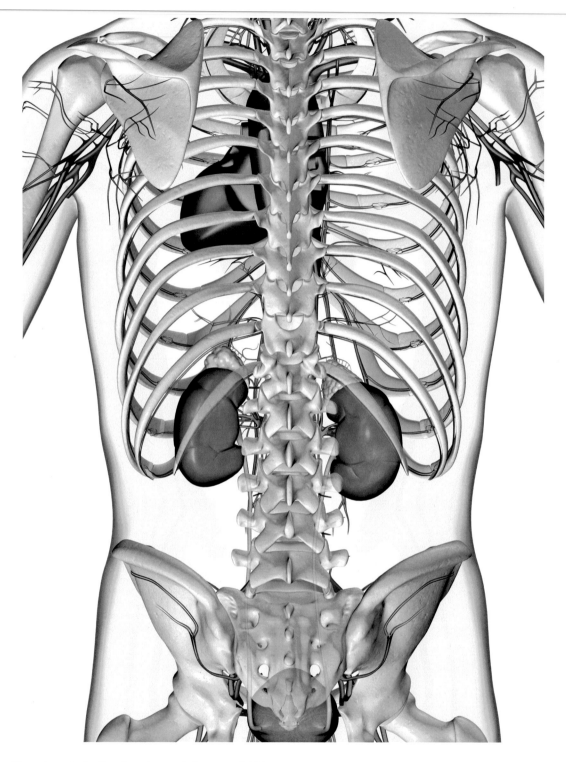

The adrenals (yellow) are located above each kidney.

foods and bodies, but we must maintain just the right amount, or cells will function poorly and can even die. The adrenal cortex makes aldosterone, which gets kidney cells to retrieve sodium from urine when sodium is getting too scarce. Aldosterone also lowers the amount of sodium lost in tears and sweat. (The kidneys also can put excess sodium into urine—thanks to atrial natriuretic factor, a hormone made by the heart.)

Cortisol is another hormone made by the adrenal cortex. A surge of cortisol is released during stress—meaning physical injury, strenuous physical work or exercise, or even strong emotional upset, fear, or shock. That cortisol surge gets fats and sugars out of cellular storage and into the bloodstream. In some people who are frequently stressed by anxiety, overwork, or emotional problems, cortisol can stay excessively high for days, weeks, or longer. Then it can be harmful, because it dampens immune cell activity, making illnesses caused by germs more likely.

Cortisol is a hormone that affects the way the body uses and stores fats and sugars. Medications similar to this hormone can be used to treat problems like allergic reactions.

ANIMAL ORGANS AND EARLY DISCOVERIES

Some of the earliest discoveries about the endocrine organs came from experiments on animals. Perhaps the earliest discovery, centuries ago, was that removing the testes of an animal, a process called castration, made the animal less aggressive, disinterested in mating, and unable to produce young. (Castration of men, too, has been a common practice in several societies over the centuries.) Experiments that removed other endocrine organs from animals had a different result: the animals died. But when substances extracted from the removed organs were given back to the animals, they survived longer. This meant that something in the organs was essential for life. Because many animals have organs similar to those of humans, these experiments shed some light on our own inner workings.

The French scientist Theophile Bordeu, in the early 1700s, described the idea of substances made in one part of the body influencing another part. A British scientist and doctor, Thomas Addison, in the mid 1800s, noticed that several of his patients had similar symptoms. After they died, he saw that each had diseased adrenals. He had discovered a deadly endocrine illness caused by poor adrenal function, now called Addison's disease. After many more years of study by curious biologists, doctors, and chemists, we have a much better understanding of endocrine organs and their actions.

Adrenals also make "sex steroids," hormones that are important in creating male and female appearance. But the amounts of sex steroids normally made by the adrenals are small in comparison to what a man's testes and a woman's ovaries make.

The adrenal medulla makes two hormones, epinephrine and norepinephrine (originally called adrenalin and noradrenalin). These hormones are the same chemicals some neurons make elsewhere in the body, including in the brain, to keep a person alert and energized. They make the heart pump faster and stronger, and breathing faster and deeper. They also help get stored sugars and fats into the bloodstream rapidly, as glucagon and cortisol do.

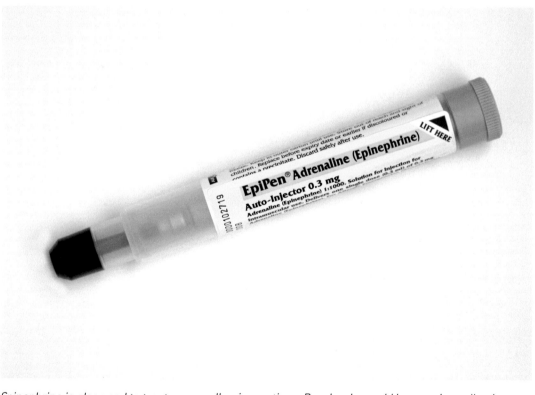

Epinephrine is also used to treat severe allergic reactions. People who could have serious allergic emergencies often carry around epinephrine stored in a pen-shaped tube. These EpiPens can be used to quickly inject the hormone when it is needed.

HORMONES FOR THE NEXT GENERATION

The hormones made by a woman's ovaries and a man's testes are not essential for life, but they *are* essential for the *next* generation's life—that is, for creating a baby. Each month, a woman's pituitary hormones, FSH and LH, cause a surge in estrogen and progesterone, made by her ovaries. Working together, all these hormones cause an egg (or sometimes more than one) to mature and leave its ovary—a process called ovulation—and travel to the uterus (womb). If the egg becomes fertilized by a sperm from a man, it will settle into the womb and begin its development into a baby over the next nine months. During that time, a mother's reproductive hormones remain quite high, and are essential for keeping the womb enriched with blood vessels. Also, the placenta forms, connecting the baby's bloodstream to that of the mother's womb. Life-giving nutrients from the mother's bloodstream support the baby's growth. The placenta makes several, plentiful hormones, too.

If an egg that leaves the ovary is not fertilized (as is the case most months), it will pass through the womb and leave the woman's body. Her hormone levels fall. Because of this, a layer of the womb that is rich in blood vessels is shed for a few days. That is called menstrual flow. But hormones levels are soon on the rise again, repeating the monthly cycle.

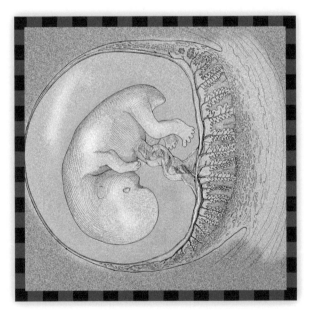

A fetus (center) is connected to the placenta (right) by an umbilical cord. The placenta provides nutrients for the growing fetus. It also produces hormones that can affect the fetus's development.

FEMALE SEX HORMONES

A pair of organs in the lower part of a woman's abdomen, the ovaries, make eggs. They also make the hormones estrogen and progesterone. Each of these influences many cells in the body to create female features, such as breasts and a fertile womb (uterus) in which a baby can grow.

The ovaries are under the control of two pituitary hormones, FSH and LH. Their quantities change throughout a month's time. For about a week they are quite low, then they rise and get quite high. The ovaries' hormones, rise and fall in response to the pituitary's hormones. This monthly pattern

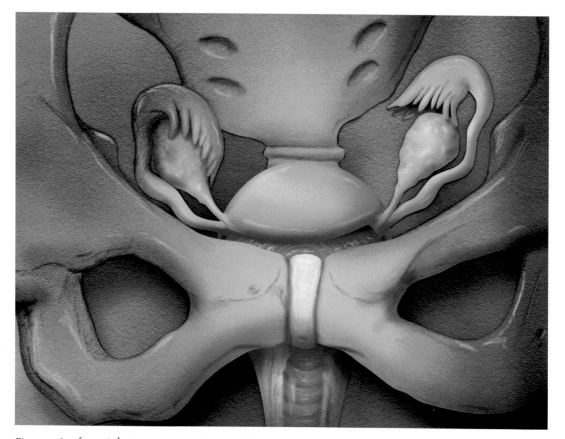

The ovaries (purple) store a woman's eggs. Hormones control when the ovaries release eggs. Hormones also control how the uterus—another part of the female reproductive system—grows and sheds its linings.

in amounts of hormones is called the menstrual cycle. It happens month after month, year after year, for many years. These hormonal cycles are what cause an egg (or sometimes a few) to grow and mature each month during a woman's reproductive years.

MALE SEX HORMONES

A man's testes are outside the abdomen, on either side of the penis, in a pouch of skin called the scrotum. (The testes and scrotum together are often called testicles). Testes make sperm, the tiny cells that can fertilize a woman's egg to make a baby. But testes also make hormones. Their most well known hormone is testosterone. Like the ovaries' hormones, testosterone is made under the control of the pituitary. But, unlike a woman's monthly hormonal cycles, a man's testosterone levels are quite similar throughout each month. This is because in a man LH and FSH from the pituitary do not increase and decrease each month, as those of a woman do.

Testosterone also causes male features, such as facial

Normal Anatomy

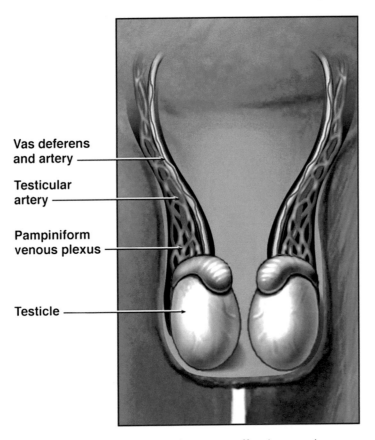

Vas deferens and artery

Testicular artery

Pampiniform venous plexus

Testicle

Male sex hormones affect how much sperm is produced in the testicles.

hair (the ability to grow a beard), hair on the abdomen, a larger larynx (voice box, visible on the front of the neck as the "Adam's apple"), a deeper voice, and larger muscles. Later in life, testosterone is what makes many men lose hair on top of their heads, while still getting more elsewhere on their bodies. Testosterone is essential for healthy sperm and to make the fluid (semen), which carries sperm.

BEYOND THE MAJOR ORGANS

Endocrine organs—as well as other organs in the body—make and use almost too many hormones to list. In addition to endocrine hormones and organs, a host of other endocrine cells are working hard to keep us alive. These cells reside in the

Male sex hormones also control hair growth in men. As boys get older, their sex hormones direct hair growth on the face and in other places around the body.

digestive tract, liver, kidneys, thymus, placenta, and many, many other places. Additionally, most of the body's cells make chemicals that travel a very short distance to influence neighboring cells—the bloodstream is not involved. These chemicals are just as important as hormones are in cellular communication and control. The endocrine organs, hormones, and cells work together to keep us in good health. However, the endocrine system can also get in the way of good health when it stops working properly.

KEY HORMONES AND THEIR MAIN ACTIONS

HORMONE	WHERE IT IS MADE	WHAT IT DOES
Growth Hormone	pituitary	Stimulates body growth.
ACTH (adrenocorticotropic hormone)	pituitary	Controls adrenal glands' release of hormones, especially cortisol.
TSH (thyroid-stimulating hormone)	pituitary	Stimulates the thyroid gland to release T3 and T4.
FSH (follicle-stimulating hormone)	pituitary	Controls hormone production by ovaries and testes; supports egg and sperm production.
LH (luteinizing hormone)	pituitary	Controls hormone production by ovaries and testes; supports egg and sperm production.
Prolactin	pituitary	Stimulates milk production in women; helps create healthy sperm in men.
ADH (antidiuretic hormone)	pituitary	Causes kidneys to conserve water that would be lost in urine.
Oxytocin	pituitary	In women, causes milk to flow from breasts while a baby is nursing; tenses muscles of the uterus (womb) during birth to push out the baby.
Melatonin	pineal	Helps cause a sense of sleepiness at nighttime.

HORMONE	WHERE IT IS MADE	WHAT IT DOES
T3 and T4	thyroid	Helps all cells stay active by using food particles for energy.
Calcitonin	thyroid	Lowers the amount of calcium in blood.
PTH (parathyroid hormone)	parathyroids	Increases the amount of calcium in blood
Insulin	pancreas	Lowers the amount of sugar and other food particles in blood after a meal by helping cells store the particles.
Glucagon	pancreas	Increases the amount of sugar in blood between meals by helping cells release stored food particles.
Aldosterone	adrenals	Causes kidney cells to save sodium from being lost in urine.
Cortisol	adrenals	Helps cells release stored food particles.
Estrogen	ovaries	Creates female appearance and maintains a healthy uterus during pregnancy.
Progesterone	ovaries	Maintains a healthy womb during pregnancy.
Testosterone	testes	Creates male appearance and helps make the fluid (semen) that carries sperm.

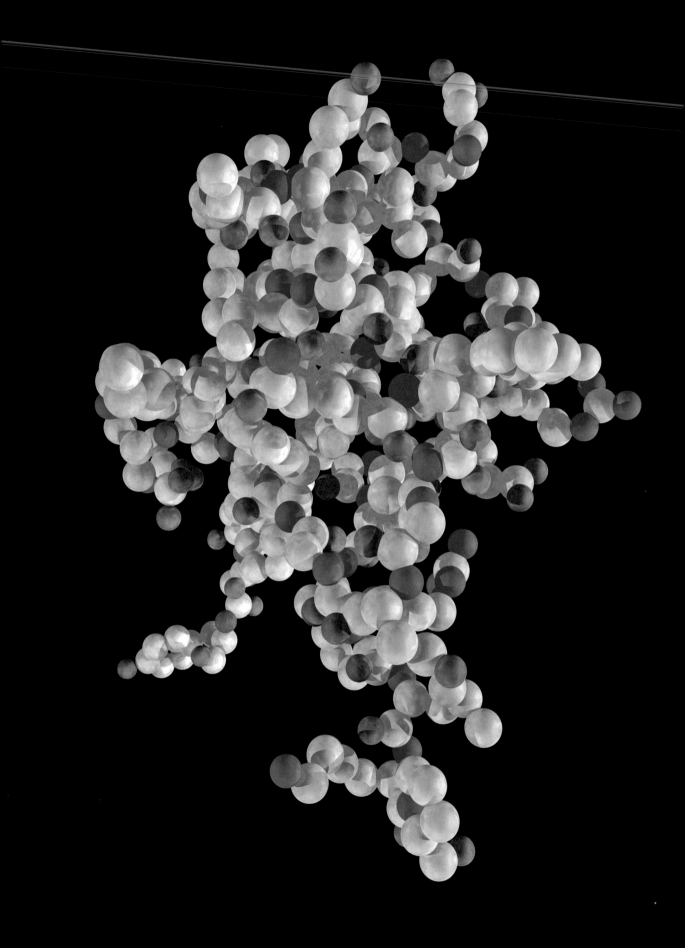

When the Endocrine System Fails

3

M ost of the time, the endocrine system carries out its many jobs quite well. But sometimes things go wrong. An endocrine organ can stop working properly. It might not make enough of its hormones or it might make too much. Some of these problems are simply annoying for a while, but others are life threatening.

INJURY

Most endocrine organs are within the abdomen, protected by layers of muscles and the ribcage or pelvis (hip bones). Others, such as the hypothalamus, pituitary, and pineal, are sheltered within the skull.

Some problems with the endocrine system—such as a lack of hormones— can be fixed when a doctor prescribes special medication. Sometimes the medication contains additional hormones or hormone-like substances.

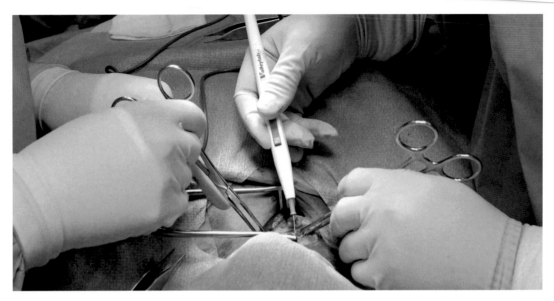

When disease or injury occurs, doctors are sometimes forced to remove part of or all of an endocrine organ. This patient is having part of his thyroid removed. The doctors will prescribe special medication that will help his body with the activities that his thyroid usually carries out.

Still, they can be injured, such as in a car accident. Then the organs will not make hormones very well until they are healed. The adrenals, ovaries, and testes come in pairs, so if one is injured, the other can carry out the work of two.

Doctors can give medications to replace hormones while an injured organ is recovering, or if it never recovers. Some of those medications are the exact hormone a person would make, while others are similar versions taken from animals. Hormones that are very simple in chemical composition can even be made in the laboratory.

PITUITARY DWARFISM

If the pituitary is badly injured, it may stop functioning, which is a life-threatening situation. Fortunately, this rarely happens. The organ is well protected deep within the brain, surrounded by the skull. But sometimes the pituitary simply makes less of a certain hormone than is normal.

Growth hormone (GH) is an example. This hormone helps people grow taller and larger during childhood, until they reach adult height. Of course, people of some ethnic groups tend to be shorter, and some taller. These differences are part of the variety within the human race. Where GH is a concern is when a child is much shorter compared to most children of the same age in her or his ethnic group. There are many reasons this might happen. Among them is a pituitary that does not make much GH. A person with pituitary dwarfism, as this condition is called, looks to be in the right proportions—their arms and legs look the right length compared to how tall they are. They are just very short.

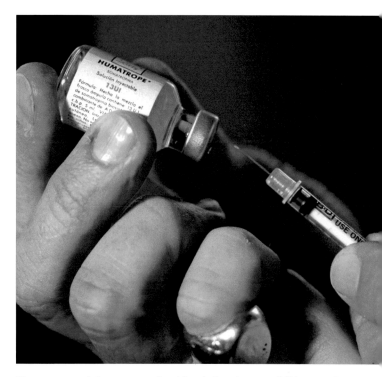

Human growth hormones should only be given to children under a doctor's supervision.

If a child is not growing as much as would be expected, GH supplements can stimulate normal growth if taken before bones stop growing. This is usually in the late teens or early twenties. There continues to be controversy related to giving children growth hormones. While it is necessary in some cases, some experts are finding that many parents are requesting hormone treatments for the wrong reasons. For example, some parents want their average-sized child to be taller or stronger in order to do better in athletics or to be as tall as the child's other siblings or relatives. Whenever growth hormones are given, doctors and parents must examine all possible outcomes and the effects the hormones will have on the child's health and well-being.

MISSING IODINE AND GOITER

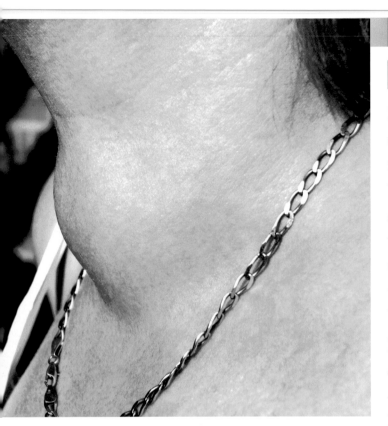

Some goiters can be small, while other can be very large and noticeable.

If someone develops a lump on the front or side of the neck, a thyroid is usually to blame. Goiter is the term for an enlarged thyroid. It can get to be as big as a baseball or even larger in severe cases. And though an enlarged thyroid can be due to cancer, most often the problem is in production of the gland's hormones, T3 and T4. And the most common cause of production problems is too little iodine in the diet. This condition is fairly common around the world. A part of the Midwestern United States where iodine in the soil is scarce used to be called "the goiter belt" because cases were so common. For the most part, iodine supplements are now used to correct this.

How is iodine related to goiter? T3 and T4 have iodine in them. When a person does not get enough of that mineral, the thyroid makes its hormones anyway, though they do not work properly. The pituitary cells that control thyroid activity perceive that there is not enough normal T3 or T4 in the bloodstream. So they release more TSH (thyroid-stimulating hormone) into the bloodstream. In response, the thyroid makes more (abnormal) hormone. Soon the gland enlarges with overactive cells and accumulating hormone.

Many cells suffer without normal T3 and T4. They are not getting the boost of help to create and use cellular energy. Muscles weaken, energy drops, thinking is foggy, digestion slows, skin thickens, and body temperature edges down. And without T3 and T4, a newborn infant cannot develop well, and may have permanent mental difficulties and physical deformities. That is why newborns should be tested for thyroid hormone levels, and given supplements if needed.

DIABETES MELLITUS

The most common health problem of the endocrine system is a condition known as diabetes mellitus. It is estimated that about 7 percent of people in the United States have this illness. That is about 21 million people. The condition is often simply called diabetes. (There is a much less common condition, diabetes insipidis, which is quite different and is called by its full name.)

There are actually two different types of diabetes mellitus. Both have to do with the hormone insulin and how it helps us fuel our cells with the food we eat. The main job of insulin is to help cells take sugars out of the bloodstream after a meal, and store them for later. The amount of insulin in the blood goes up shortly after a meal or sugary snack because food particles pass through the pancreas, activating its cells to release a surge of insulin. In response to the insulin, fat cells, liver cells, and muscle cells speed up their activities to store away food particles—especially sugars. But this process goes wrong in diabetes mellitus. Cells cannot take in sugars, so the sugars accumulate in the bloodstream.

In type 1 diabetes (also called insulin-dependent diabetes), sugar accumulates because the pancreas does not make insulin. In most people with this condition, the insulin-making cells were there at birth, but at some point during childhood—often in the early teen years—the cells

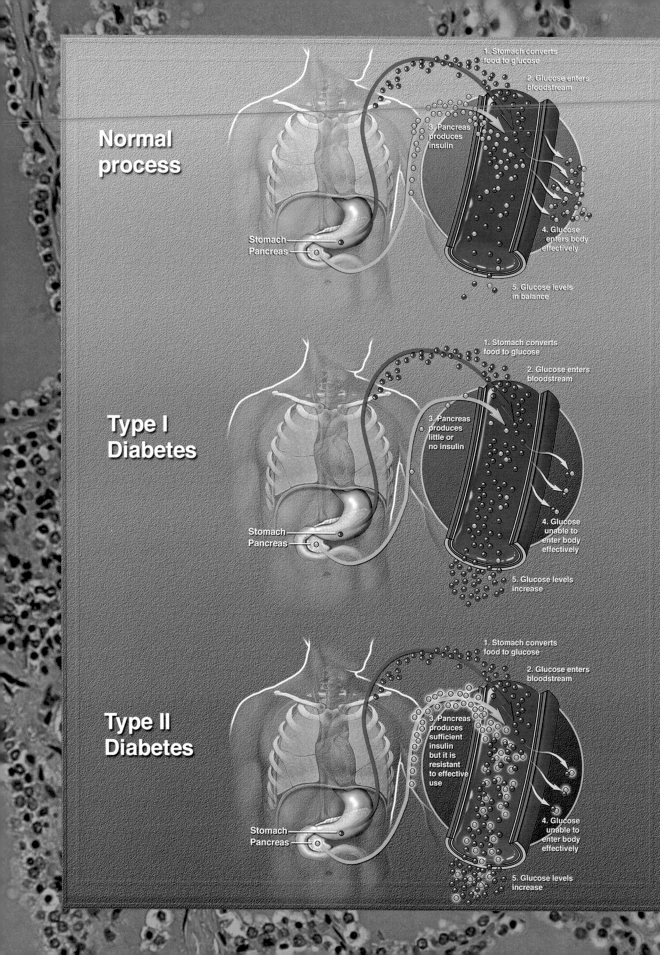

were destroyed. Why this happens is still being studied, but it seems likely that the body's own immune system mistakenly attacked them. This may have happened because certain types of germs or viruses settled among pancreas cells. People with type 1 diabetes must have an injection, or a shot, of insulin once or several times daily to help control sugar levels in their bloodstreams.

In type 2 diabetes, the pancreas makes insulin, but sugar still builds up in the bloodstream. The problem lies instead in the target cells, which are the cells that should store away the food particles. These target cells have lost their ability to react to insulin. Why? Most people with type 2 diabetes have gained a lot of weight because of overeating for many months or years. This means that their cells have been handling a lot of sugary, fatty foods and beverages for a long time. The cells have been exposed to a lot of insulin, and eventually ignore it. These cells make fewer and fewer receptors where the insulin can attach. It is similar to how we stop noticing the sound of a humming computer or refrigerator after a while.

People of all ages can develop type 2 diabetes if they are overweight, do not have a healthy diet, and do not exercise regularly. Families who exercise regularly and eat right have a better chance of staying healthy.

SUGAR IS NOT ALWAYS SWEET

Diabetes mellitus is the most common disorder of the endocrine system. It causes sugars to accumulate in the bloodstream because cells are not doing well at taking sugars in, or storing them away. What is wrong with too much sugar in the bloodstream? High levels of sugar make it more likely that a number of health problems will arise. Sugar sticks to the insides of blood vessels, changing their surfaces and injuring them.

Over time, important organs such as the heart, kidneys, and eyes become damaged due to a poor blood supply. Heart attacks and blindness are more common in people with diabetes than people without the disorder. Also, when hands and feet are cut or injured, they may not heal well and may become infected with germs. The infections may spread to the arms or legs. Sometimes, these parts of the body must be removed, or amputated, to keep the infection from spreading to vital organs and becoming deadly.

People with type 1 diabetes, who make no insulin to control sugar levels, have another risk. They can suffer from a buildup of chemicals called ketones. The ketones are a byproduct of fats and proteins that are being used by cells for energy, since sugars are not being used properly. These ketones change the body's chemistry and can cause a sudden coma (unconsciousness). The coma can be fatal without immediate medical attention.

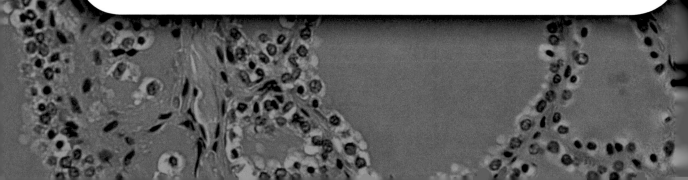

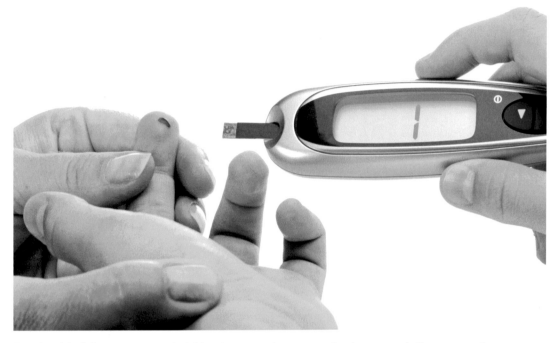

People with diabetes can test their blood sugar at home, at school, or at work. Easy-to-use instruments prick the skin and then collect blood. Within seconds, the person can find out if their blood sugar is too high or too low.

Type 2 diabetes is far more common than type 1 diabetes, and is becoming even more prevalent in the United States. Some health experts call it an epidemic. This is because more children are greatly overweight than ever, and adults are getting heavier, too. The good news is that—in most cases—type 2 diabetes can be reversed, unlike type 1 diabetes. Target cells can go back to making more receptors and responding to insulin properly. The cure is to eat better foods with fewer calories and get more exercise, in order to lose weight gradually and healthfully. Insulin supplements or other diabetes drugs may be needed for a while to boost the chances that cells will respond a little better.

SEX HORMONES

Hormones from a woman's ovaries (estrogen and progesterone) and a man's testes (testosterone) are not essential for life. Still, these so-called sex hormones are important for good health because many cells respond to them. Bone, blood vessel, brain, skin—all seem to work best with normal amounts of these hormones. These hormones also influence a person's appearance. It is the hormones from a woman's ovaries that make her body shape and facial features look different from a man's. Similarly, a man's testosterone causes his physical features to be different from a woman's. Additionally, each gender needs proper hormone amounts in order to make healthy sperm or eggs.

Each person makes hormones in slightly different amounts. Some make a little more of the sex hormones, others make less. This is normal. For instance, a man might have less facial hair and be less muscular if his testosterone amount is on the low side of average. However, this does not necessarily mean that he has an endocrine or hormone problem.

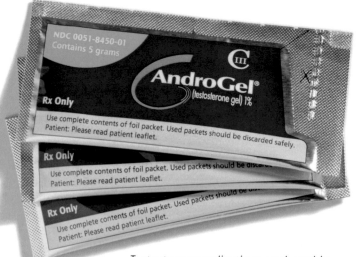

Testosterone medications, such as this androgen gel, can be given to men who are not producing enough of the hormone.

In some instances, though, hormone levels become too low for proper development or reproduction. A very low testosterone level can mean smaller genitals—penis and testicles—because these parts of the male body require testosterone to grow during puberty. A woman, too, might have an especially low amount of estrogen or progesterone in her bloodstream. Of course, a

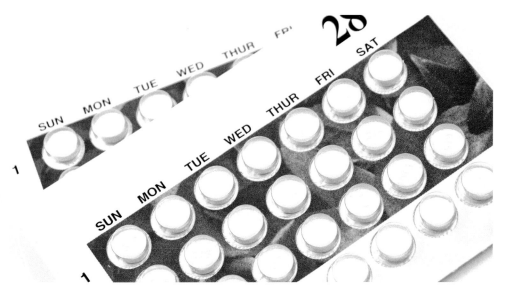

Birth control pills are a type of hormone therapy that women use to regulate their body's sex hormones and menstrual cycle.

woman's hormone amounts rise and fall each month, but even during the "high" times, these hormones could be too scarce to keep her healthy. This can happen to women who exercise a huge amount and eat too little, so that they are very thin. This also happens for women and girls with eating disorders and who are very underweight. Without enough nourishment, their ovaries stop making hormones, and menstrual cycles cease until they gain some weight. If necessary, supplements of sex steroids, taken under a doctor's care, will raise blood levels to the normal range.

GETTING BACK TO NORMAL

Some of the problems discussed here are simple to correct with a healthy diet and exercise. Others can be corrected by medical help, which could include taking hormone supplements. But it is important to remember that variation in hormone amounts among people is normal. Hormones levels change as the body changes. It is when the levels are too far from normal that health issues arise, and medical help may be necessary.

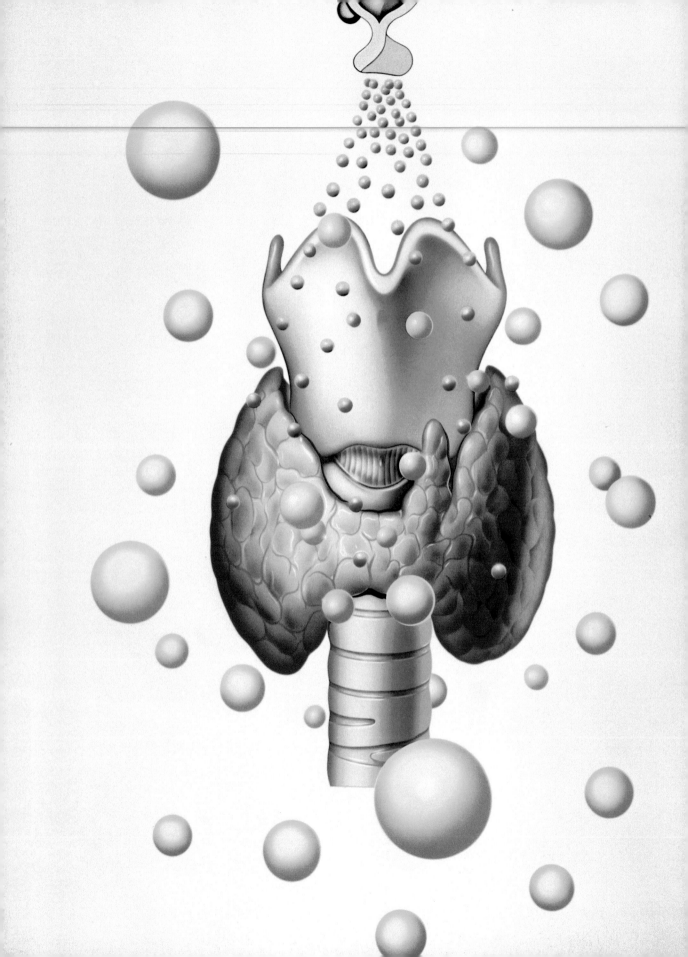

4

When the Endocrine System Does Too Much

The endocrine system is supposed to make just the right amount of hormones to keep everything running smoothly. Thankfully, it usually does just that. But sometimes there is too much of a hormone in the bloodstream. When that happens, health problems may arise. They can be minor problems that are simply annoying, or much more serious— even life-threatening.

PITUITARY TUMORS

Anything that goes wrong with the pituitary can cause trouble with other endocrine organs. That is because the pituitary controls several

Many illnesses and disease are caused when the thyroid—and other endocrine organs— release too many hormones.

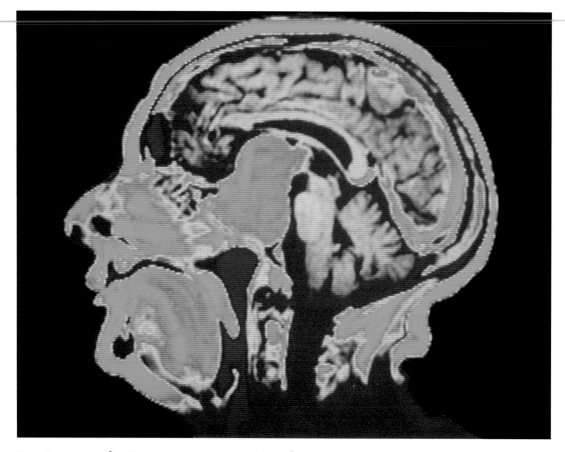

A pituitary tumor (in blue near the center of the brain) has damaged the pituitary gland and other brain structures near it. Pituitary tumors cause hormone imbalances or diseases like Cushing's syndrome.

endocrine organs. If the pituitary puts out too much of its hormones, any cells that normally react will do so even more. For certain cells, that reaction is "Make more of your hormones!" In this way, the pituitary can cause excesses in the hormones made by other endocrine organs, such as the thyroid, adrenal, ovaries, and testes.

The most common reason for a pituitary to make too much of something is a tumor—a collection of extra cells. A tumor in the pituitary might be made of thousands or millions of cells. If those cells are busy making a hormone, they will add to what the pituitary is already putting into the bloodstream.

Tumor cells often do not pay any attention to how much hormone the body needs. This is different from normal pituitary cells, which adjust how much hormone they make depending on what is already in the bloodstream, and what the body needs at any moment.

Growing Big

The pituitary's growth hormone (GH) makes a person's muscles and bones grow, especially during puberty. Some people make far more growth hormone than the average person, and grow especially tall. It is hard to say what "too tall" is, and there is nothing wrong with how much GH most people make. But in some cases, there is a tumor in the pituitary that is making GH. This can cause gigantism, a condition where a person grows very rapidly during puberty and early adulthood. Such a person may get as tall as eight feet or more!

Sometimes too much GH is made all throughout adulthood, long after puberty's growth spurt has ended. This leads to a slow, continual growth

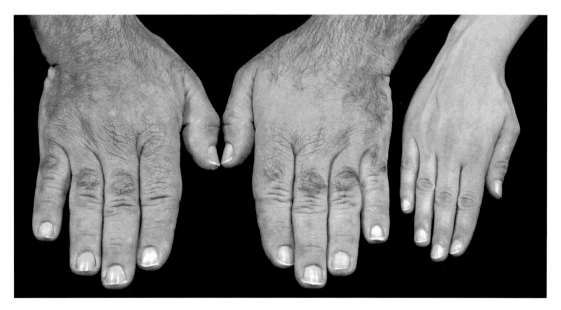

Acromegaly causes a person's body to grow to abnormal proportions. The hands on the left belongs to a man with acromegaly. The hand on the right belongs to a woman of the same age who does not have acromegaly.

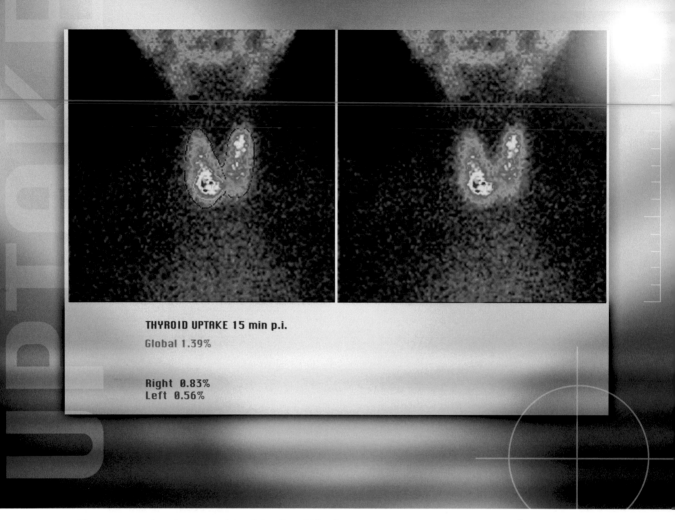

THYROID UPTAKE 15 min p.i.

Global 1.39%

Right 0.83%
Left 0.56%

These scans show how one side of the thyroid (yellow and red colors indicate activity) is more active than the other side. An overactive thyroid can lead to a number of illnesses or disorders.

of certain parts of the body, especially the hands, feet, and certain features of the skull, such as the jaw and forehead area. This condition, called acromegaly, can change a person's appearance quite a bit over his or her lifetime.

TOO MUCH THYROID ACTION

What would happen if a hormone that keeps billions of cells busily working were to become too abundant? Those cells would be very busy indeed. A person with this condition would likely have a rapid heart rate and breathing rate, be very active and jumpy, lose weight because of so much activity, or have trouble sleeping. These and other changes are symptoms of too much thyroid hormone. This sometimes happens because a group of cells have multiplied in the thyroid and are making too much hormone. It also happens if the pituitary's hormone, or something similar to it, stimulates the thyroid too much. In most cases, the actions of an overactive thyroid can be counteracted by taking medications prescribed by a doctor.

INSULIN OVERDOSE

It is rare to make too much of the hormone insulin. But a person who takes insulin as a medication may take too much. This problem is worth mentioning, because it can be very dangerous.

Insulin is given as a medication to people who do not make enough on their own. So their doctors work with them to figure out how much to

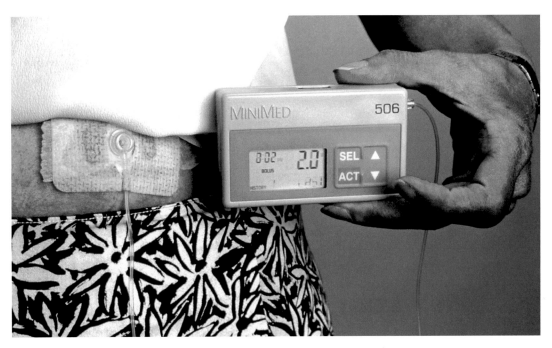

Some people who do not make enough natural insulin wear a special insulin pump. This pump automatically delivers the correct amounts of insulin whenever the body needs it.

take, and how often, so that it acts most like the body's own hormone. That is not so easy to do, because the amount of insulin in the blood normally changes minute to minute. Whatever the body needs at a certain time, the pancreas will provide. Medication, though cannot mimic that, and sometimes a dose of medication turns out to be too much.

With too much insulin, cells that respond to it get carried away. They take too much of the sugars and lipids out of the bloodstream and store them away. This is dangerous for the rest of the body's cells. What are they to use for energy if they cannot get enough food particles from the bloodstream? The answer is, not much. They slow down and do less. That is a problem especially for the brain, which can only keep working with enough sugar from the bloodstream. Low blood sugar, called hypoglycemia, can cause weakness, confusion, nausea, and loss of consciousness for a few minutes (fainting) or for hours or days (coma). Fortunately, a sugary beverage or candy can rescue the situation if these are taken early enough. If emergency medical help is needed, a sugary fluid can be injected into a vein—right into the bloodstream—to speed recovery.

CORTISOL AND CUSHING'S

Cortisol helps to get fuels to all of the body's cells when blood sugar is getting low. It does so by boosting a fat cell's ability to release its stored fats, and a liver cell's ability to release stored sugar. But cortisol can also cause muscle cells to break down some of their interior material—the proteins that make them strong—as an "emergency" fuel source in the bloodstream. Protein from skin and bones may be used, too. All of these actions can, over time, make a person thin, weak, and unhealthy.

These effects of excess cortisol are especially apparent in people with Cushing's syndrome. Weakened muscles and loss of fat from the arms

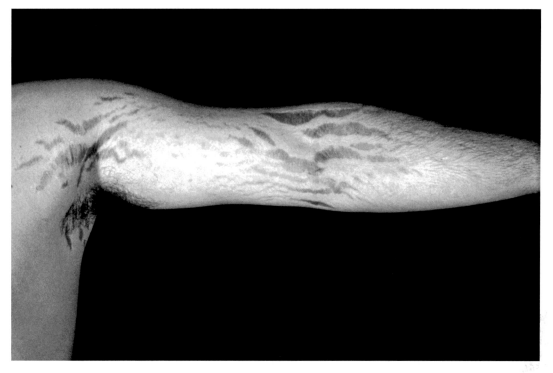

Symptoms of Cushing's syndrome may include large stretch marks across a person's skin.

and legs makes them especially slender, though fat may linger and even increase around the abdomen. Skin is easily bruised and heals poorly. Bones break more easily. The face is quite round, and probably means another adrenal hormone (aldosterone) is too high also.

Cushing's syndrome may be due to a pituitary tumor that makes a lot of ACTH. That hormone's usual task is to stimulate the adrenal to make cortisol. Too much ACTH means too much cortisol. Or, a genetic problem may be to blame. (Cushing's is common in people with Down syndrome, who have an extra chromosome). Certain medications that are similar to cortisol can also cause physical changes similar to Cushing's syndrome. If a doctor determines that a person has Cushing's, he or she may prescribe special hormone medications to help. If the Cushing's is caused by a tumor, cancer treatments like radiation or chemotherapy may also be given.

In women, too much male sex hormones can cause a lot of changes in the body. However, sometimes women bodybuilders purposely take male sex hormones—like testosterone—to build up more muscle. They may develop larger muscles, but these women will also be more likely to develop masculine features and can also damage their bodies with hormone abuse.

PROBLEMS WITH SEX HORMONES

It is not usually a problem for a woman to have too much estrogen or progesterone, or a man to have too much testosterone. But an excess of the *opposite* hormone for one's gender can alter some of the features that make a person look like either a man or a woman. The truth is, every person makes some of each kind of sex hormone—male and female. But women normally make much more estrogen than testosterone. And men normally make much more testosterone than estrogen. But that can change.

A woman with an abundance of testosterone, or a similar male sex hormone, may develop facial hair, prominent muscles, bone enlargement, enlargement of her genitals, and a deep voice. She probably will stop having menstrual cycles and making eggs. A tumor in the woman's adrenal is a common cause of this. The adrenal normally makes certain chemicals similar to testosterone, but only in small amounts. A tumor can make quite a lot. Surgery to remove the tumor often reduces the amount of male hormone, and returns the woman's features to female ones. Women who take muscle-building steroids, which are like testosterone, may have those same changes. But sometimes her male features remain even after she stops taking the steroids.

A man with excess estrogen will loose some of his male features. He may lose facial hair, develop small breasts, and stop making sperm. Excess estrogen in a man is rare, but certain chemicals used in factories, plastics, farming, and raising meat animals are similar to estrogen. Some scientists suspect that these are causing the decrease in sperm production and ability to father children that has been noted around the world in the last few decades.

5

Building a Good Endocrine System

The human body is a wondrous thing. It can learn all sorts of physical skills, such as dancing, typing, swimming, and climbing sheer cliffs of rock. It can repair itself from many kinds of injuries and illnesses. It even grows and changes, and yet stays similar enough that you can recognize a person year after year.

To do all this, we must pay attention to how we care for ourselves. For instance, to keep our muscles well toned, we should exercise them. But what about keeping the endocrine system well toned? You cannot really "exercise" this body system, other than by letting it do its job. Still, here are some points to keep in mind so your hormone-making cells remain healthy.

The endocrine system plays a part in most of the cellular activities that go on in your body. Without this system you would not have enough energy to move around.

SAY NO TO UNNECESSARY HORMONE SUPPLEMENTS

Your body makes hormones in extremely small amounts. A very tiny bit goes a very long way. In fact, hormones are present in the bloodstream in such tiny amounts that they went unnoticed for centuries until chemists invented ways to find chemicals in amounts too small to be measured by other methods.

But nowadays, you can get highly concentrated forms of certain hormones. Anabolic steroids are an example. They are testosterone-like hormones that increase muscle growth in both men and women. They continue to be used by athletes to boost performance, even though they are banned and illegal to purchase unless prescribed for a medical condition by a doctor.

Anabolic steroids have unpleasant and dangerous side effects. In a woman, anabolic steroid abuse can lead to male features, such as jaw growth and facial hair. Some side effects may even be fatal. In fact, some young and fit athletes have suddenly died of a heart attack—a suspected problem with anabolic steroids. These hormones also are known to increase aggression and violence among men. Additionally, anabolic steroids flood the pituitary

Though they may enhance athletic performance, abusing anabolic steroids is very dangerous for the body.

with a message of "plenty of testosterone around." As a result, the pituitary does not signal a man's testes to make his own testosterone. Soon his genitals begin to shrink and his testes stop making sperm. (The anabolic steroids do not keep genitals healthy, as natural testosterone does.)

Taking melatonin supplements without a doctor's supervision is another example of using hormones that may cause damage to your body. Melatonin is sold—legally, so far—as an aid for jet lag, which is the exhaustion that follows traveling through different time zones. It seems that melatonin may "reset" the

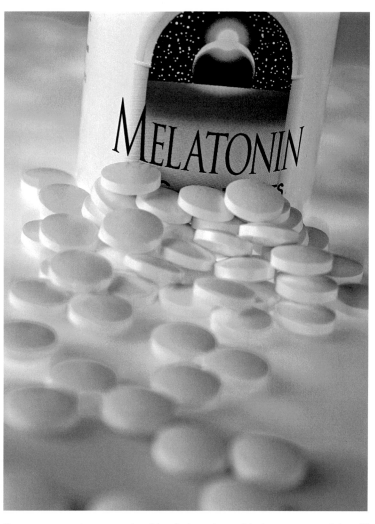

Hormone supplements should only be taken with doctor supervision. If you think you have a hormone imbalance, a doctor can run tests, determine what the problem is, and prescribe a safe method of treatment.

sleep-wake cycle for a person who has crossed several time zones while flying. But melatonin is fairly new as a supplement. It has not been available long enough to know what problems high doses might cause. But taking any hormone in an amount larger than its normal range should be done very carefully. Or better still—not at all, unless there is a medical reason to do so, and a doctor to help supervise.

HORMONES AS MEDICATION

Hormones are sometimes given as medication to improve a health problem. Here are examples of hormones commonly used as medication, and why.

HORMONE	PROBLEM	WHAT THE HORMONE DOES
Insulin	Diabetes mellitus, in which sugar in the blood is too high.	Lowers blood sugar by helping cells store it away.
GH (growth hormone)	Very small height during childhood due to producing less GH than normal.	Causes growth to an average height (or nearly so).
LH (luteinizing hormone)	A woman cannot become pregnant.	Stimulates ovaries to make many eggs, which may help a woman get pregnant.
T3 and T4	Deformed or inactive thyroid gland since birth.	Allows normal development of a baby, which would have many physical and mental problems without enough T3 and T4.
	Low hormone amounts because of old age or thyroid cancer.	Allows normal activity and energy levels, both for individual cells and for the whole body.
Cortisol-like hormones	Swelling, itching, or pain that becomes excessive or life-threatening, such as from allergies.	Reduces the activities of cells that cause swelling, itching, and pain.

EAT NUTRITIOUS MEALS

How many times have you been told to eat nutritious meals? One reason is exactly related to endocrine system: diabetes. It is clear that someone who is very overweight is much more likely to get type 2 diabetes. That, in turn, ushers in a whole set of health dangers. Changing one's diet to cut out a lot of sugars and packaged (processed) foods is not that hard, especially when good-tasting grains and interesting vegetable dishes are added. There are many guides in books and on the Internet about how to eat well—and have fun doing it—to avoid diabetes type 2. A doctor or nutritionist is also a good resource for eating right. An endocrine system that has been harmed by excess body weight can often recover if more healthful habits are practiced.

Drinking too much soda and other sugary drinks can lead to health problems like diabetes. A healthy diet will help keep all your body systems working smoothly.

A healthy diet should include a variety of fruits and vegetables. Vitamins and minerals found in these foods are good for many endocrine organs.

MOVE THAT BODY

All our cells run on fuel and oxygen from the bloodstream. But sitting around does not get blood flowing very well. To really deliver what your cells need, get some activity throughout the day. Even just a five-minute walk, or some dancing, or helping in the yard, or cleaning the house is exercise. Whatever gets your body moving, gets your blood flowing. Exercise also uses up some stored food particles (in fat cells) and so, in small steps, can healthfully bring weight down to a normal range.

Simple physical activities that get your heart pumping will help you stay healthy.

BE GOOD TO YOUR BODY

By now you have probably learned that some things just are not that good for your body. You know that inhaling things such as smoke, gasoline fumes, burning plastics, and spray paint, can damage the throat and lungs. But inhaled substances also cross into the bloodstream and are carried to cells, including those of the endocrine system. There, they may harm cells, or trigger mutations, or changes, that could lead to tumor growth. Drinking too much alcohol harms the liver—an organ necessary to control hormone levels.

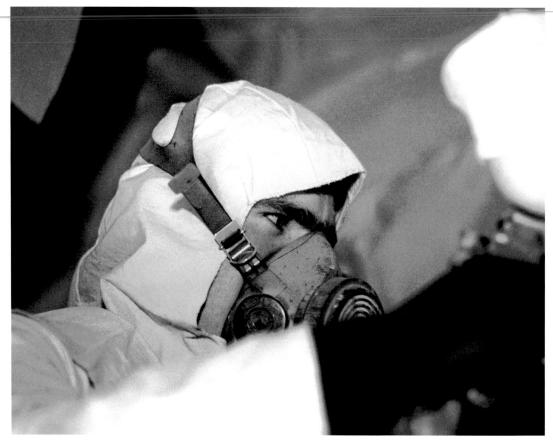

Proper protective gear should always be warn when handling dangerous substances.

LEARN ABOUT POLLUTANTS AND TOXINS

People are wondering more and more whether manmade chemicals are harming our bodies. Several chemicals of concern are similar to sex steroids, especially estrogen. These chemicals may be getting into foods from plastic wrap and plastic containers, especially when heated. Pesticides, industrial chemicals, and even some food additives are suspected of being "endocrine disruptors"—meaning that they are harming the normal functioning of hormones. Studies show that some wild animals are not developing and maturing properly, and some are not able to breed. Researchers worry that hormone-like chemicals are harming humans, too.

What can you do? Try not to keep or heat food in plastic, especially fatty foods, which combine with plastics better than other foods. Keep beverages in metal or glass containers. Choose foods with the least man-made ingredients. Eat organic foods that are free of pesticides whenever you can. Wash nonorganic fruits and vegetables well.

While some pesticides and fertilizers help sustain larger crops, those chemicals can also make a person sick. Always wash fruits and vegetables before eating them. If you are worried about pesticides and other chemicals, do some research about where your food comes from and how it is grown and handled.

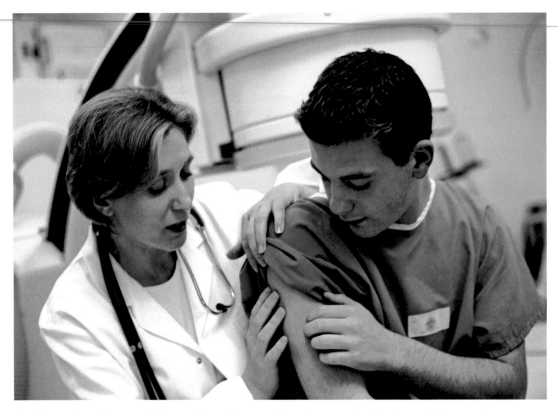

Besides eating right, exercising, and watching out for toxins, regular check-ups with your doctor are also important.

You can also look for news and tips about what kinds of chemicals might be harmful, and try to avoid them. Remember, the endocrine system still holds a lot of mysteries. We all have much more to learn about how it works—including in relation to the world around us, not just within us.

abdomen—The area of the body between the chest and the hips.

adrenal glands—The pair of endocrine organs in the abdomen that make several hormones, including aldosterone, cortisol, androgens, and epinephrine/norepinephrine.

ACTH (adrenocorticotropic hormone)—The pituitary hormone that stimulates adrenals to make aldosterone.

ADH (antidiuretic hormone)—A pituitary hormone that prevents kidneys from losing too much water in urine.

aldosterone—A hormone of the adrenals that gets kidneys to save sodium.

cortisol—A hormone of the adrenals that ensures there are energy sources in the bloodstream for cells to use, especially during times of physical or emotional stress.

eggs—The cells made by a woman's ovaries that combine with sperm to make a baby.

endocrine cells—The collection of cells throughout the body that make hormones.

endocrine system—The body's team of endocrine cells and their hormones, which work together to control much of what the body does.

enzymes—Substances that facilitate chemical reactions.

epinephrine/norepinephrine—Two very similar hormones made by the adrenals that are also important chemicals controlling the nervous system.

estrogen—One of the hormones of a woman's body, made by her ovaries, that allows her to make eggs and to look like a female.

FSH (follicle stimulating hormone)—A pituitary hormone that stimulates ovaries and testes to make their hormones and to make eggs or sperm.

gland—A structure of the body that produces a substance, usually as a liquid.

glucagon—A hormone of the pancreas that increases sugars in the bloodstream.

gonads—The parts of the body that make eggs or sperm, which come together to make a baby. In women, the ovaries are the gonads. In men, they are the testes.

growth hormone (GH)—A pituitary hormone that stimulates growth during childhood years.

hormone—A chemical made by one type of cell that travels in the bloodstream to influence the behavior of another type of cell.

hypothalamus—A part of the brain right near the pituitary that controls much of the pituitary's activities.

insulin—A hormone of the pancreas that reduces sugars, fats, and proteins in the bloodstream.

LH (luteinizing hormone)—A pituitary hormone that stimulates ovaries and testes to make their hormones and to make eggs or sperm.

melatonin—The pineal gland's hormone, which helps a person feel sleepy each night and may have other important tasks.

metabolism—The process by which substances are broken down by cells to create energy or nutrients.

ovaries—The pair of organs in a woman's body that make eggs.

pancreas—An organ in the abdomen that makes digestive enzymes as well as the hormones insulin and glucagon, which control the quantities of food particles, especially sugars, in the bloodstream at any moment.

parathyroid glands—Four tiny endocrine organs within the thyroid, which help control the body's amount of calcium.

pituitary gland— An endocrine organ located inside the brain. It produces hormones that control growth, reproduction, metabolism, and other bodily functions.

progesterone—One of the hormones of a woman's body, made by her ovaries, that allows her to look like a female and prepares her womb to nourish a developing baby.

sex hormones (reproductive hormones)—The hormones made by ovaries (estrogen and progesterone) and testes (testosterone) that make women and men look different, and able to make eggs or sperm.

sperm—The cells made by a man's testes that combine with an egg inside a woman's body to make a baby.

T3, T4—Abbreviations for the thyroid hormones, which contain 3 or 4 iodine atoms.

target cell—A cell that reacts to a hormone.

testes—The pair of organs in a man that make sperm.

testosterone—The hormone in men that allows them to appear male, and to make sperm.

thyroid—An endocrine organ in the throat area that helps control the amount of calcium in the body and, makes thyroid hormones which all cells need to stay active.

Find Out More

Books

Haney, Johannah. *Juvenile Diabetes*. New York: Marshall Cavendish Benchmark, 2005.

Olien, Rebecca. *The Endocrine System*. Mankato, MN: Capstone Press, 2006.

Shannon, Joyce Brennfleck. *Endocrine and Metabolic Disorders Sourcebook*. Detroit, MI: Omnigraphics, 2007.

Walker, Pam and Elaine Wood. *The Endocrine System*. San Diego: Lucent Books/Thomson Gale, 2003.

. . . .

Web Sites

Endo 101: The Endocrine System

http://www.hormone.org/endo101

Endocrine System

http://www.vivo.colostate.edu/hbooks/pathphys/endocrine/index.html

Endocrine System—A Body Basic's Article

http://www.kidshealth.org/teen/your_body/body_basics/endocrine.html

Your Gross and Cool Body: Endocrine System

http://yucky.discovery.com/flash/body/pg000133.html

Bibliography

American Diabetes Association. "All About Diabetes." American Diabetes Assoc. http://www.diabetes.org/about-diabetes.jsp

Cowley, Geoffrey. "Melatonin." *Newsweek*, August 1995, http://www.mtnhigh.com/newsweek.html

Dryden-Edwards, Roxanne. "What Is Seasonal Affective Disorder (SAD)?" MedicineNet, Inc. http://www.medicinenet.com/seasonal_affective_disorder_sad/article.htm

Environmental Research Foundation. "Sperm in the News." http://www.ejnet.org/rachel/rehw477.htm

History of Endocrinology: http://science.jrank.org/pages/2469/Endocrine-System-History-endocrinology.html

Marieb, Elaine N. *Human Anatomy and Physiology*. 6th ed. Redwood City, CA: Benjamin Cummings, 2003.

Ohlsson, Claes, Bengt-Åke Bengtsson, Olle G. P. Isaksson, Troels T. Andreassen, and Maria C. Slootweg. "Growth Hormone and Bone." *Endocrine Reviews* 19, no. 1 (1998): 55-79: http://edrv.endojournals.org/cgi/content/full/19/1/55

Seasonal Affective Disorder: http://www.kidshealth.org/teen/your_mind/feeling_sad/sad.html

Springhouse. *Pathophysiology Made Incredibly Easy!* 3rd ed. Philadelphia: Lippincott Williams & Wilkins, 2006.

Wright, Lawrence. "Silent Sperm." *The New Yorker*, January 15, 1996. http://www.converge.org.nz/pirm/ssperm.htm

Index

About the Author

Lorrie Klosterman is a science writer and educator who earned a Bachelor of Science degree from Oregon State University and a Doctoral Degree from the University of California at Berkeley, both in the field of zoology (the study of animal life, including humans). She has taught courses in human health and disease to college and nursing students for several years, and has written about health for magazine's. Lorrie Klosterman has also written several health-related books for young adults. Her greatest joy comes from experiencing and learning about the amazing world of animals and plants, and sharing those experiences with others.